ARCO-AIRCAM AVIATION SERIES

B-25B Mitchell flown by Lt. Col. James Doolittle on the Tokyo raid of the 18th April 1942. The sixteen B-25's took off from the deck of the USS Hornet at 8.20 a.m. ship's time. Standard OD and grey scheme US ARMY on underside of wings, red centre to all insignia. Central turret removed and replaced with extra 50 gallon fuel tank.

NORTH AMERICAN B-25A/J MITCHELL

IN USAAF·USMC·RAF·FREE FRENCH·NEIAF KON.MARINE & FOREIGN SERVICE

Compiled by Richard Ward

Illustrated by Richard Ward and Michael Roffe

Text by Ernest R. McDowell

ACKNOWLEDGEMENTS

This book on North American's Mitchell, the first American aircraft to take the war to the Home Islands, flying from the deck of the *Wasp*, would not have been possible without the assistance of many friends whose names are listed below in alphabetical order, my thanks to all. Peter M. Bowers, R. A. Brown, J. Cuny, d'E. C. Darby, ECA, Groupe Lorraine, Hugo Hooftman, IWM, B. van der Klaauw, E. R. McDowell, North American, S. P. Peltz, R.Neth.AF, Frank F. Smith, USAF, US Marines.

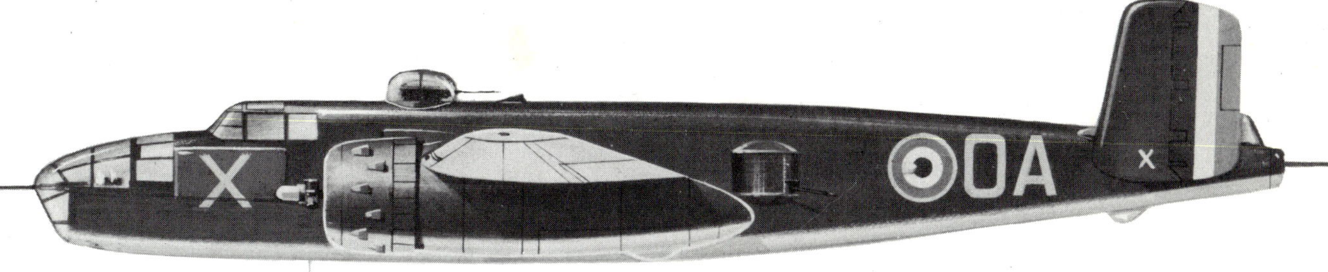

Mitchell II No. 342 "Lorraine" (Free French) Squadron, RAF, in standard OD and grey scheme as side view illustration F1.

PUBLISHED BY

Arco Publishing Company, Inc., 219 Park Avenue South, New York, N.Y. 10003

First Published by Osprey Publications Ltd., and Printed in Great Britain

Library of Congress No. 77-113958 · SBN 668-02312-0

A very interesting photograph of a Marine PBJ-1D Mitchell on its way home after bombing Japanese installations on Matupi Island, once powerful naval base guarding the entrance to Rabaul Harbour. The smoke is rising from supply dumps set on fire during this raid and can be seen trailing from them over the city of Rabaul situated on the bay to the right of the main crater in foreground. (US Marines)

A formation of B-25H Mitchells of the 1st Air Commando Group flying through monsoon clouds en route for targets in Burma in support of Chindit operations. (USAF)

NORTH AMERICAN B-25A/J MITCHELL

North American Aviation's Model NA-40 was conceived as a result of a 1938 Army Air Corps requirement for a twin-engined attack bomber. The design proved to be an unsuccessful one in the competition, but when another Army proposal was issued in 1939 for a twin-engined medium bomber, North American brought out the NA-62. This was simply a redesign of the NA-40 to meet certain new specifications called for by the Army.

The NA-40 had been an all metal high-wing monoplane with a low-slung tricycle landing gear which gave it a squat appearance on the ground. The co-pilot was seated behind the pilot in a greenhouse that was reminiscent of the old Martin B-10. A large glassed-in nose section provided the bombardier-navigator with ample room to operate his bombsight and the single .30 calibre Browning machine gun provided for defence against frontal attacks. Additional guns were proposed, with four fixed .30's in the wing plus a mid-upper position in the fuselage, as well as a gun mounted in the floor to the rear of the ship. Five hundred rounds per gun were provided for and provision for 1,200 pounds of bombs in several combinations of weights and sizes completed the armament. Powered by two Pratt & Whitney R.1830-S6C3-G Twin Wasps rated at 1,100 horse-power each, the plane had a top speed of 265 miles per hour and grossed out at 19,500 pounds. Fuel capacity was 476 gallons.

A successful first flight was made in January of 1939 with North American test pilot Paul Balfour at the controls.

The design team of R. H. Rice and J. L. Wood now set to work to redesign the entire aircraft to meet the new specifications given them by the Army. The result was model NA-62 which differed quite a bit from the original design. Over 8,500 new engineering drawings plus almost 200,000 man hours of engineering work went into the NA-62.

To obtain additional tank and bomb stowage space they raised the top of the fuselage and faired the crew's cockpit into its upper contour. They also moved the co-pilot next to the pilot. This actually improved the aerodynamic design. The wing was lowered to a mid-point configuration from the old shoulder position. The new wing attachment point made for a better main spar location and at the same time altered the general aspect of the plane. The Wright R-2600-A71 Cyclone engines used on the NA-40-2 were replaced by Wright R-2600-9 engines developing 1,700 horse-power each, and the nacelles were extended aft of the trailing edge of the wing. An enlarged tail section permitted the addition of a .50 calibre Browning as a "stinger" in that area. The size of the crew increased from three to five.

The Army Air Corps accepted the design "right off the drawing board" and no X or Y aircraft were required. The acceptance took place on 10 September 1939 and on the 20th an order was placed with North American for 184 B-25's, the new designation assigned to the design by the Army. The advent of war in Europe had figured in the quick acceptance and the waiving of the usual experimental models and service test aircraft. The first flight of the B-25 took place on 19 August 1940.

Widening the fuselage to accommodate the co-pilot and new bomb stowage positions as well as increasing the wing span one and one half feet to 67 feet 6 inches caused some problems during flight tests conducted at Wright Field. Directional stability during the bomb run was a bit on the marginal side. Excessive dihedral was suspected and the outer wing panels were re-rigged to an absolute horizontal setting. This produced the "gull wing" look that was to become characteristic of the B-25 series, and it also cleared up the stability problem.

The first modification, which produced the B-25A, was dictated by aerial combat reports filtering in from Europe and consisted of simply adding self-sealing fuel tanks and armour plating protection for the pilots. This was incorporated into the 25th production airplane. All told forty B-25A's were delivered to the Air Corps during 1941.

About this time the B-25 received a popular name—

the Mitchell. The aircraft was named in honour of Brig. General William "Billy" Mitchell, the pioneer airman who was the champion of the bomber and its place in the war in the air.

The next model in the series, the B-25B, was quite extensively re-designed. The tail "stinger" was eliminated and two powered turrets were added in the dorsal and ventral positions. Both turrets featured twin .50 calibre Brownings. The upper turret carried 600 rounds per gun while the lower turret carried 700 rounds per gun. The ventral turret was fully retractable, the guns fitting into slots in the belly of the plane. Sighting was done through a periscope by a kneeling gunner. The Air Corps took delivery of 119 of the B-models before the change over to the C-model took place.

The B-25-C-NA was the first of the Mitchells to be really mass-produced. When the final C-model rolled off the production lines it was the 1,619th built. The C had an auto-pilot installed and under-wing bomb racks fitted. It also had the more powerful R-2600-13 engines installed. A second production line was set up in Kansas City to supplement the original North American line at Inglewood, California, and this new centre turned out 2,290 examples of the B-25D-NC, which was basically the same aircraft as the C-model. Naturally, in such long production runs many small changes and modifications were made. The C series ran from the C-1 through the C-25NA, while the D-series ran from the D-1 to the D-35NC. These variants had a number of new items installed, such as provision for ferry tanks in the bomb bays, individual exhaust stacks attached to each cylinder with special exit fairings incorporated into the cowl skirt section, auxiliary wing tanks, a .50 calibre Browning replacing the .30 in the nose, and in some cases the lower turret was eliminated.

Ten of the B-25D's were modified for use as photographic reconnaissance aircraft and were designated the F-10. All armament was removed and extra fuel tanks were installed. Cameras were mounted in the rear fuselage and in a chin fairing under the nose in a tri-metrogen arrangement.

Two B-25C's were converted into an XB-25E and an XB-25F to test de-icing systems for the tail and wings. These were the first B-25's to bear an X designation but neither proved successful and they were abandoned. Another B-25C was modified to become the XB-25G and proved to be a qualified success. General Kenney was promised 63 of these aircraft but didn't really want them. The G-model was unique in that a regulation Army 75 mm. cannon was surmounted in the nose. The M-4 used weighed just over 900 pounds sans ammunition. It was nine and one half feet long and the cradle mounting extended under the pilot's seat. The nose was foreshortened on the G-model and faired around the cannon's muzzle. The gun recoiled 21 inches when it was fired, and, as one pilot put it, "Stopped the plane in mid-air and then shoved it a couple of feet backwards, while you prayed that the whole thing wouldn't simply exit through the tail". The shells weighed 15 pounds apiece and twenty-one were carried. The navigator now became a cannoneer, as it was his job to slam the shells into the breech. When the G reached the Southwest Pacific, General Kenney placed the first one in the hands of his chief "Gadgeteer", Lt.-Col. Paul I. "Pappy" Gunn, who put it through the course. "Pappy" liked the 75 mm. but wanted more firepower, so he added four forward firing .50's in blisters alongside the nose of the fuselage. These were in addition to the two already mounted in the nose of the G.

"Pappy's" new baby was beset with problems. After test firing about 350 rounds from his packages the skin of the plane began to ripple and tear away around the bomb bay. Cracks appeared along the leading edge of the wing between the fuselage and the nacelle. The primary structure was also weakened by the vibration and blast effect. The problem was taken to "Pappy's" favourite people at the 4th Air Depot in Townsville and the "technicians" came up with the solution. The defects were corrected by beefing up the structures at the critical points. All told ninety-seven additional parts were used in the process. Fifty-two sets of them were fabricated to order by the 4th A/D Group to "Pappy's" specifications.

Speed fell to 281 m.p.h., and while the 75 mm. gun was very effective when hits were scored it placed the crews at a distinct disadvantage in that the aircraft had to be held on a straight and level course in order to sight and fire the weapon. While the nose machine guns were used to suppress flak and also to line up the cannon they could not take out all the flak and as a result the airplane was often a sitting duck for the anti-aircraft gunners off to the side of its flight path.

When Kenney had agreed to take the G-models it was with the understanding that he could modify them in the field if necessary, and after being used for a time in the New Britain area and the Marshalls he ordered the cannon removed. Each plane then received two .50's to

Good side-view of the NA-40, predecessor of the Mitchell.

Another view of the NA-40, note the high-wing position and very low ground clearance. (Photos North American)

NA-62, a comparison with the above photos will show the points of major re-design, notably fuselage, wing position and undercarriage. (North American)

Nice flying shot of one of the early B-25's. Only nine were built with this wing geometry, subsequent aircraft were modified to what became the familiar "gull" configuration. (North American)

replace it. North American produced a total of 405 of the G-model.

The B-25H came along in 1943, and the modifications were inspired mainly by the successes of "Pappy" Gunn's boys in the V Bomber Command. This new version retained the 75 mm. cannon in the nose but was equipped with the newer and lighter T13E1 type. Four .50's were added in the nose section at the North American factory, and "Pappy's" packages were added to the sides. Twin .50's were mounted in a power-operated tail stinger in the redesigned tail section, and one .50 was installed in the waist position on each side of the ship. The dorsal turret was moved forward on the fuselage to a spot just behind the cockpit. The lower turret was eliminated. It had proved to be more of a hindrance than an asset, as more often than not it would be rendered useless by hydraulic fluid or dust on the sight. The H-model had a total of fourteen "big fifties" plus the cannon. It was also equipped to carry a one-ton torpedo or 3,200 pounds of bombs. The crew strength remained at five, but new duties resulted. The pilot and co-pilot remained but the navigator was also a radio man and a cannoneer, the two gunners in the waist positions were also a flight engineer and a camera man, while the tail gunner alone was a career gunner with no other job.

North American decided to remove two of the "fifties" in the nose, and the co-pilot as well, and in this space install a cabin heater. This was fine with the boys in cold regions but was not acceptable to Kenney and others in desert areas, where it never got cold or where they operated on the deck. The co-pilot could be a great asset if the pilot should be wounded or killed on a mission.

An oddity in production came about in the H-series, as production was terminated on the 1,000th aircraft in favour of the new J-model; there was no I-model in between, as the Air Force did not use the letter I in series to avoid confusing it with a 1.

The B-25J was the last of the B-25's and it was also the most numerous model. A total of 4,318 were completed before production stopped with the war's end. The J-model returned to the original concept of the Mitchell, and the bombardier and his greenhouse were restored. The nose now contained two fixed and only one movable .50 calibre machine guns. Crew now stood at six. The J was quite similar to the H in other respects.

Other designations

The R.A.F. accepted a number of Mitchells from the U.S.A. under lend-lease, and these received British designations. The Mitchell I was the mark applied to the B-25B, and a total of 23 were supplied. The Mitchell II included both the B-25C and the B-25D models, and a total of 533 were sent to the R.A.F. The Mitchell III was the same as the B-25J, and the R.A.F. received 314 of them.

The U.S. Navy received a number of B-25's and they were operated by the U.S. Marines as PBJ's. The 706 that were turned over to the Navy for the Marines were designated as the PBJ-1, PBJ-1C, PBJ-1D, PBJ-1G, PBJ-1H, and PBJ-1J, with the letter following the -1 indicating the B-25 model in the original series.

The R.C.A.F. received a few Mitchells which they used under the British designation.

The F-10 photographic reconnaissance version has already been mentioned. The final designations were assigned to a number of war-weary Mitchells which found their way into use as advanced trainers. These were the AT-24A, B, C and D, and they corresponded to the B-25D, G, C and J in that order. Later all advanced trainers were given a TB designation and these then became TB-25's.

Foreign service

The R.A.F. was the first foreign nation to receive the B-25 and use it in combat. The first to reach England was the Mitchell I, which was used only for flight training and familiarization and did not see any combat use.

The Mitchell II was sent to No. 2 Group to equip No. 180 and No. 98 Squadrons, which were soon up to operational standards. The first R.A.F. Mitchell raid took place on 22 January 1943, just about three and a half months after the Mitchells arrived in the U.K. As more arrived they were turned over to the 2nd TAF and were soon being operated by Nos. 342, 305 and 320 Squadrons, the latter being an all-Dutch outfit flying with the R.A.F. after the fall of their homeland. When the Mitchell III's arrived they were sent as replacement aircraft to the units in the 2nd TAF. Used mainly in the tactical rôle. these squadrons did an excellent job throughout the war.

The Red Air Force received a total of 870 B-25's during the war, but not much has been published regarding the use of the Mitchells in Soviet service. They seem to have been used mostly in an attack rôle by the Russians against tactical targets.

The Brazilian Air Force received twenty-nine B-25's which were used mostly in anti-submarine and patrol work during the war. The Canadians received only four Mitchells while the war was on, and none were used in combat.

The Dutch took delivery of 249 B-25's under lend-lease, and besides the squadron operating with the R.A.F. they had No. 18 Squadron operating with the R.A.A.F. The majority of the Dutch Mitchells operated in the Southwest Pacific Area during the war.

The last nation to receive and operate B-25's during the war was Nationalist China. A total of 131 Mitchells went to the Chinese Air Forces under lend-lease arrangements. The entire 1st Bomb Group of the Chinese-American Composite Wing was equipped with the B-25 by 1944.

In summing up the Mitchell one can say that it was one of the outstanding twin-engined aircraft of the war. It was easy to fly, readily adaptable to a number of rôles, and subjected to endless modifications, most of which were successful. The crews liked it and so did the men who had to keep it flying. It was an honest aircraft and certainly earned its niche in aviation history.

Combat operations

The Southwest Pacific Area Theatre of Operations was the one in which the B-25 probably did its greatest job. Four of General Kenney's V Bomber Command Medium Bomb Groups were equipped with various models of the B-25. These were the 3rd, 22nd, 38th and 345th Groups. The 71st Recon Group also flew some B-25's with the 5th Air Force. The four bomb groups between them were awarded nine Distinguished Unit Citations, two Congressional Medals of Honor, and four Philippine Presidential Citations.

The Third Bombardment Group was fondly known to every one as the "old Third Attack Group", as it dated back to 1919 in its history. The Third played a large rôle in the sinking of a Japanese convoy in the Battle of the Bismarck Sea, and won its first DUC at Wewak on 17 August 1943; by pressing home the attack in the face of intense enemy flak the group destroyed a large number of aircraft on the ground during repeated strafing runs.

On 2 November 1943, the Third Group again went down on the deck to hit a concentration of enemy shipping in Simpson Harbour, New Britain. Major Raymond H. Wilkins led his 8th Squadron in on a skip-bombing run and personally sank two *Marus*. Out of bombs, he continued to make repeated runs on a parallel course to the other Mitchells in his squadron to draw the enemy fire away and enable them to run true. His ship was hit, lost a wing, hit the water and exploded. His gallant action resulted in the posthumous award of the Congressional Medal of Honor for his bravery.

The 22nd Group, after switching to B-25's in October 1943, wasted no time in learning how to use them most effectively; they were awarded a DUC for knocking out enemy entrenchments with their new Mitchells on 5 November 1943.

Above: A pair of early B-25A Mitchells. (P. M. Bowers)

Below: Line-up of B-25B's in OD and grey scheme with insignia in six positions, US ARMY on wing under surfaces. (North American)

Below: Nose detail of a B-25C, note the two fixed ·5's in the nose offset to starboard.

Below: F.10 (B-25D) of an unknown Carribbean based unit. (USAF)

Above: B-25G with two fixed ·5's in the nose plus a 75mm, serial is 265189. OD and grey scheme with red surround to insignia. (USAF)

Above: B-25H resplendent in highly polished natural metal. (USAF)

Above: B-25J, this shot shows to good advantage the package guns, tail position and wing insignia. (USAF)

Below: Another B-25C, this view shows the exceptionally clean lines of the type. (USAF)

Factory fresh B-25H awaiting delivery to a USAAF unit, serial 34198 in yellow, red surround to national insignia, OD and grey scheme. (USAF)

The 398th Squadron of the 22nd Group was sent to knock out some tanks on Wadke, but while *en route* these were destroyed by the ground forces. The 398th could have aborted the mission but instead went in on those long, straight runs demanded by the 75 mm.'s to shoot up some gun emplacements. The flak was intense and every ship in the formation was hit, one fatally, but they continued their runs until the emplacements were wiped out.

The 38th Group sent its ground echelon to Australia while the air echelon remained in the States for additional training; two squadrons *en route* to join the Group in Australia arrived in Hawaii just in time to become involved in the Battle of Midway, but never did rejoin their Group afterwards. They were replaced by others. The 38th went into combat while based in Australia and moved up to New Guinea later. On 18 August 1943 a large raid was scheduled to hit a concentration of Japanese aircraft at Wewak. Sixty-two Mitchells took off and fifty-three reached the target area. The enemy had been alerted and the ground fire was heavy. Major Ralph Cheli was leading his flight from the 405th Squadron when his B-25 was hit by a mixed gaggle of Zeros and Oscars. One Oscar in particular was giving the entire flight trouble; after shooting up one of the others he turned his full and undivided attention to Cheli's B-25. Soon the right engine was on fire and the flames spread to the wing, but with the target area in sight Major Cheli coolly held his place in the line and led the flight across the strip, blasted a line of Zeros parked on the flight line, then radioed for his wing man to take over just as the B-25 rolled over, spun into the sea and blew up. Major Cheli was posthumously awarded the Medal of Honor for the mission.

The 38th staged another large raid to Hollandia in conjunction with the 345th Group, the "Air Apaches", in June of 1944. Taking off from the staging field at Hollandia after having bomb-bay tanks fitted and filled, they headed for the twin airfields of Jefman-Samate on what was at the time the longest mission ever flown by B-25's. Arriving over the Jefman strip at 12.55 hours on 16 June 1944 the 38th caught the Japanese by surprise as they came in line abreast formation almost at grass-top level. The fighters which attempted to get off were gunned down, and the 100-pound parafrag bombs rained down and ripped up planes and men alike. Continuing on their way, they caught the troops at Samate and repeated their act. Surprised defenders could only manage a belated barrage, but did manage to catch one of the "tail-end Charlies" and shoot him down. This was the only loss suffered on the mission, while the 38th claimed 11 enemy fighters destroyed in the air; the 345th claimed only a lone Hamp as destroyed, while bemoaning their fate as the second wave in the attack. There just wasn't much left for them after the 38th got there.

The 38th picked up four DUC's winning them at Papua, New Britain, New Guinea and Leyte, which was a record among the B-25 Groups in the V Air Force.

The last B-25 Group in the 5 Air Force was the 345th Bomb Group, known as the "Air Apaches". The 345th was perhaps the most colourful group so far as markings were concerned in the entire war. The 345th won a DUC for carrying out a number of attacks on enemy targets at Rabaul on 2 November 1943. The "Air Apaches", as mentioned, were colourful in the decorations applied to their Mitchells. On the fin and rudder, most painted the Group insignia, which was an Apache Indian head. Some carried the head of a wild horse on the fin and rudder, but it was the nose that really received their full attention. Hawk heads, panther heads, tiger heads, clown faces, bat heads, insect heads—name it, and one of the B-25's probably sported it. The four squadrons also had colourful names; the 498th were the Hawks, the 499th the Bats Outa Hell, the 500th the Mustangs, and the 501st the Black Panthers.

In closing the B-25 story in the Southwest Pacific Area the 71st Reconnaissance Group must be mentioned, as they operated a number of B-25's, and while their main task was to provide the command with target and damage assessment photos they also bombed and strafed as the occasion arose.

The name of "Pappy" Gunn must rank high whenever the Mitchell is mentioned, as he more than any other man was responsible for much of its success in the SWPA, and his gadgets and modifications were the basis of a new type of aerial warfare. Other names that belong on any roll of honour connected with the B-25 would have to include Col. John P. Henebry, Col. Fay R. Upthegrove, Col. Jarred V. Crabb, Col. Chet Coltharp, Col. Glen Doolittle, and Major Ed. Larner.

European Theatre

The Mitchells in the E.T.O. flew a total of 63,177 sorties, dropped 84,980 tons of bombs and destroyed 193 enemy aircraft in aerial combat. Against these totals they lost 380 planes in combat. Used entirely in a tactical rôle, they went after targets that were smaller in size and against which the big bombers were not really fully effective from the standpoints of both accuracy and economy of effort. Their targets required just as much guts to hit, as much bombing accuracy, and they usually took as much flak over their targets as the big boys did.

The Mitchell groups operating in Europe were those which initially had been in the 9th and 12th Air Forces in North Africa and had moved across to Italy to continue the war. These included the 12th and 340th, which were in the 9th Air Force in Africa and were then transferred to the 12th Air Force when the 9th went back to England. The 12th was a bit unusual in that it eventually found its way to the 10th Air Force in India. Other groups operating with the 12th included the 321st and the 310th.

The only B-25 outfit to serve with the 8th Air Force in England was the 25th Bomb Group (Reconnaissance), which flew a mixed group of aircraft including the Mitchell on aerial recon flights over the waters adjacent to the British Isles.

As a sample of the B-25's use, the 12th Group while in the Western Desert Campaign flew 91 missions totalling 744 sorties, and dropped 1,536,000 pounds of bombs while losing 10 aircraft in combat. They claimed two enemy aircraft destroyed in aerial combat.

The four groups won a total of seven DUC's during their tours. The 12th won theirs for continuing action in North Africa and Sicily rather than for any single outstanding mission. The 310th won its first DUC for a raid on marshalling yards at Benevento in Italy despite fierce enemy opposition from flak and fighters. The second was won when they held a very tight formation to knock out the bridge at Ora despite a virtual carpet of flak thrown at them by the Germans. The 321st also collected a pair of DUC's getting one for a raid on an airfield near Athens, and a second for hitting a battleship, cruiser, and submarine in the harbour at Toulon. The 340th got its first DUC for supporting the British Army in Tunisia as well as Allied Forces on Sicily, and received number two when they sank a cruiser in the heavily defended harbour at La Spezia.

Miscellaneous service

The 7th Air Force had a single Mitchell group assigned to it, the 41st Group, which started from Hawaii and island-hopped to Tarawa, Eniwetok, Makin; returned to Hawaii and worked up on the new rocket-carrying B-25's; and then went on to Okinawa. The group attacked shipping and tactical targets but spent most of its tour harassing the Japanese in the by-passed Marshalls and Carolines.

The 10th Air Force picked up the 12th Bomb Group as mentioned previously, but also had the 341st assigned. The 341st received the nickname of "The Burma Bridge Busters" after Maj. Bob Erdin discovered the secret of "flip" bombing by accident. Maj. Erdin, leading a raid against the bridge over the river Mu, came in low, so low that he had to haul back on the stick to avoid hitting a tree just as the bombs away was given. Much to his surprise he not only scored hits, but three spans of the bridge were collapsed and in the water when the smoke cleared. The tactic was refined and it won the group their DUC.

The 11th Air Force's single B-25 group, the 28th, won a DUC for its operations from Alaska against the Kuriles during the period April 1944 to August 1945, when the weather was as much an enemy as the Japanese.

The last combat air force to have a Mitchell group was the 13th, with its 42nd Group. The 42nd was presented with a DUC for its pre-invasion attacks on the island of Borneo in the area around Palikpapan.

There were a large number of miscellaneous training and recon units equipped in part or wholly with B-25's; some of these were the 1st Air Commandos, 1st Photo Group, 2nd, 5th, 11th, 26th, 65th, 66th, 69th, 70th, 74th, 75th, 76th, 77th (all recon training groups), and the 11th Photo Recon Group. These were attached to the 1st, 2nd and 3rd Air Forces in the ZI.

U.S. Marine Corps service

The Marines received a large number of Mitchells which the Navy designated as the PBJ-1 plus a letter designating the model. The first Marine Squadron to fly the PBJ was VMB-413, which was commissioned on 1 March 1943 at Cherry Point NAS. More squadrons were commissioned including VMB-423, 433, 443, 611, 612 and 613. These were soon overseas and in action. Each squadron consisted of 15 Mitchells and 30 crews. During the war the Marine losses were 45 aircraft and 173 officers and men, but only 26 of the PBJ's were lost in aerial combat.

VMB-612, as an example, went to Iwo Jima after it was secured and in a little over three months flew 251 sorties, hitting 53 vessels and claiming five of them as sunk. The squadron lost seven PBJ's, three in combat, during this period.

B-25B Mitchell with de-icer boots awaiting delivery to a service unit.

The Big Mission

No story about the B-25 would be complete without mentioning the mission flown by Col. Jimmy Doolittle and his Tokyo raiders. The story of the mission has been told and retold, and a number of good books have been written about it.

The raid was launched at a time when the morale of the American people was at a low ebb, and must rank as one of the epic missions of the war. What the Battle of Britain was to the British, the Doolittle raid was to Americans. Doolittle was an American hero as a racing pilot and aviator before the war, but after the raid he was almost a god to many of his countrymen.

The Tokyo raid was not a stunt; each plane had a military target, which most hit, and while it achieved little towards turning the tide of the war, it did have far-reaching effects in that the Japanese were forced from that time on to begin to think in terms of defence of their homeland. Many aircraft retained in Japan as a result of the raid were needed badly elsewhere. So when Col. Doolittle soared off the deck of the *USS Hornet* on 18 April 1942 he gave an already significant date in American history an even more important meaning, and gave the B-25 its place in history even if it had never flown another mission.

Above: Close-up shot of the pair of B-25A's, note details of the tail position and split fuselage window. (Peter M. Bowers)

Above: Late model B-25A, US ARMY on under surfaces standard for this period. (USAF)

Below: B-25A Mitchells lined-up on Biggs Field, Texas during the March 1942 War Games. (USAF)

Above: B-25A of the 17th Bomb Group, 34th Bomb Squadron, note the Thunderbird insignia on nose and blue band on cowl. (USAF)

Above & below: 17th Bomb Group B-25A's, note the glossy black prop blades, white band on cowl and Thunderbird insignia. (Peter M. Bowers)

Below: Port side shot of a 17th BG B-25A taken at a later date than those above. (Peter M. Bowers)

Above: The 10th B-25C modified with a solid nose, unit unknown. Row of five Jap flags under cockpit, name "Mortimer", serial 112443. (USAF)

Above & right: Close-up shots of two of the F-10 Mitchells in the photograph below.

Below: Formation of F-10's of a Caribbean based unit, ZZ is "Pistol Packin" Mama', see colour illustration. (USAF)

Desert camouflaged B-25C Mitchell's of the 12th Bomb Group, 82nd Bomb Squadron, 9th Air Force, heading Benghaziwards in company with RAF Desert Air Force Baltimores with an escort provided by DAF Kittyhawks. Note Kittyhawk just above turret in top picture. Lower shot shows the Libyan coastline and was probably taken crossing the Gulf of Sirte. (USAF)

Above: B-25C Mitchell of the 12th BG, 434th BS, 9th AF, USAAF, coming into land on a Tunisian airfield, probably Hergla where the group was based during June and July 1943. (USAF)

Above: B-25C Mitchell of the 12th Bomb Group, 83rd Bomb Squadron, over the Apennines heading for a target in Northern Italy.

Below: Interesting B-25C probably of the 310th Bomb Group, 12th Air Force, operating from Telergma, Algeria, 1942, shortly after the "Torch" landings. Note US flag on fin. (USAF)

Above: Fine action shot of B-25C's of the 340th Bomb Group, 487th Bomb Squadron, 9th Air Force, attacking a bridge on the Volturno River in Italy. (USAF)

Below: Believed to be the 320th Bomb Group coming in to land at either Massicault or El Bathan, Tunisia, June or July 1943. Note red surround to national insignia and white tip to fin and rudder. (USAF)

Two good shots of formations of the 340th Bomb Group on its way to attack targets in Italy. Top photo shows the 488th Bomb Squadron, note the additional starboard upper wing insignia has at this time been deleted on all aircraft. Lower photo shows the 489th BS on its way to the Anzio beachhead. The group originally flew with the 9th Air Force, being absorbed into the 12th Air Force in August 1943 when the 9th returned to the UK. (USAF)

Above: Another good shot of the 488th Bomb Squadron airborne, this time on its way to attack Cassino on 15 March 1944, 340th BG, 12th AF. Waves of medium and heavy bombers attacked every 15 minutes from 8.30 am to 2.30 pm. (USAF)

Two good shots of B-25C's of the 488th BS coming into land on a Corsican airfield early in 1944. The under surfaces of 8K are far from standard. (Peter M. Bowers)

Fine selection of photographs of a B-25G Mitchell of the AAF Tactical Center, Orlando Field, Florida. Red mouth, white teeth, red lips and blood drips; aircraft is painted in the early USAAF maritime scheme, see colour illustration. (Photo USAF)

Above: B-25H's of the 1st Air Commando Group heading out through heavy weather for targets in Burma, note the four Mustangs flying escort. (USAF)

Above: B-25H's of the 1st ACG taking off from Hailakandi in India for a raid on targets in Burma; below close-up of 2. (USAF)

Below: Line-up of natural metal B-25H Mitchells of the 1st ACG on Chittagong airfield in January 1945. See cover illustration. (USAF)

Above: B-25H of the 1st ACG leaving Jap supply dumps burning in Burma, serial is 34325. (USAF)

Below: Neat formation by the 1st ACG, nearest aircraft is 1 "Barbie III", with 6 "Dolly" next in line. It should be noted that the white fuselage stripes were rather loosely applied, on some aircraft straight down the fuselage on others in gentle curves. (USAF)

Above: Nice shot of B-25H's of the 1st ACG buzzing their home field of Hailakandi, India. 10th Air Force, China-Burma-India Theatre. (USAF)

Below: Good landing shot of a B-25J of the 12th BG, 83rd BS, 10th AF, CBI. OD and grey scheme, code on rudder 61. (Peter M. Bowers)

Above: B-25H Mitchell, 12th Bomb Group, 82nd Bomb Squadron, 10th Air Force, on an Indian airfield. (USAF)

Above: Another B-25H of the 82nd BS landing on an Indian airfield during the monsoon period, note lake due to rains in foreground. (USAF)

Above & below: Mouths and other nose decor of various Mitchells of the 12th Bomb Group, 10th Air Force, CBI. (via E. R. McDowell)

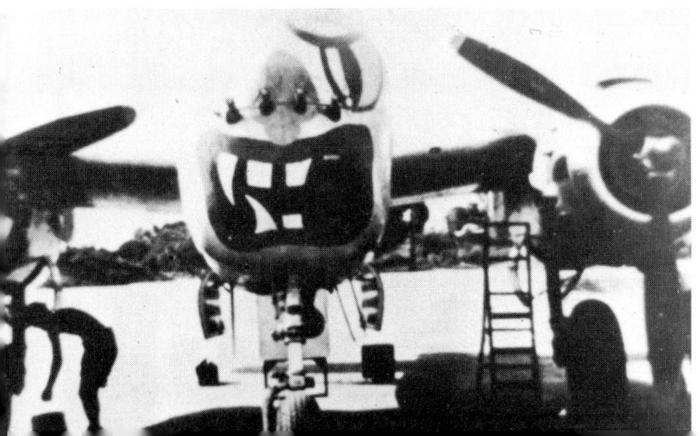

Above: B-25H, 12th BG, 434th BS, 10th AF, CBI. (Peter M. Bowers)

A pair of B-25J's of the 12th BG; upper 83rd BS, lower 82nd BS. (Peter M. Bowers)

Below: "Bones", the last B-25 to come off the production line at NA's Inglewood plant. 12th BG, 82nd BS, 10th AF. (USAF)

Above: Sharkmouthed B-25J Mitchell of the 345th Bomb Group, 5th Air Force, SWPA, attacking a Japanese convoy off Keviang, New Ireland. Note Mitchell coming in low between the masts of the cargo ship which was eventually sunk. (USAF)

Below: A B-25J Mitchell of the "Air Apaches" attacking Japanese troop concentrations and supply dumps in Humbolt Bay, New Guinea. 345th Bomb Group "Air Apaches", 499th Bomb Squadron "Bats Outa' Hell", 5th Air Force. (USAF)

Above: B-25J Mitchell, 345th Bomb Group, "Air Apaches", 499th Bomb Squadron "Bats Outa' Hell', 5th Air Force, SWPA. See colour illustration.

Left: Close-up showing the "Batmouth" insignia and armament detail of a B-25J of the 499th BS. (Photos via E. R. McDowell)

Below: B-25G of the 345th BG, 499th BS. See colour illustration.

Below: B-25C of the 345th Bomb Group, squadron unknown. Nadzab airfield, New Guinea, 1944.

Below: B-25G of the 345th BG, probably of the 501st BS, 5th AF, SWPA. Nadzab airfield, 1944. The "Tiger Head" is yellow with red mouth, white teeth, red, black and white eye with black details. (Photos via d'E. C. Darby)

A

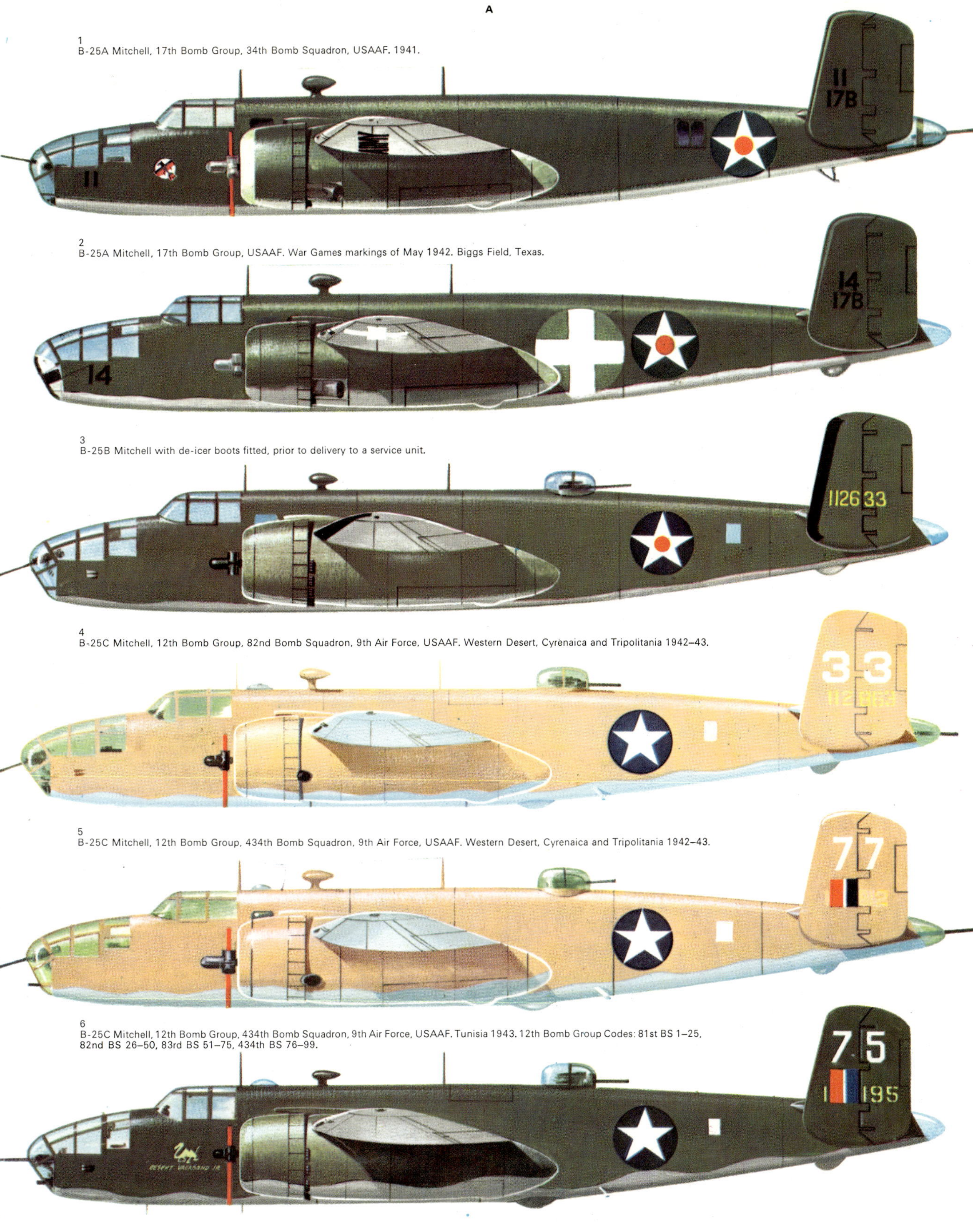

1
B-25A Mitchell, 17th Bomb Group, 34th Bomb Squadron, USAAF. 1941.

2
B-25A Mitchell, 17th Bomb Group, USAAF. War Games markings of May 1942. Biggs Field, Texas.

3
B-25B Mitchell with de-icer boots fitted, prior to delivery to a service unit.

4
B-25C Mitchell, 12th Bomb Group, 82nd Bomb Squadron, 9th Air Force, USAAF. Western Desert, Cyrènaica and Tripolitania 1942–43.

5
B-25C Mitchell, 12th Bomb Group, 434th Bomb Squadron, 9th Air Force, USAAF. Western Desert, Cyrenaica and Tripolitania 1942–43.

6
B-25C Mitchell, 12th Bomb Group, 434th Bomb Squadron, 9th Air Force, USAAF. Tunisia 1943. 12th Bomb Group Codes: 81st BS 1–25, 82nd BS 26–50, 83rd BS 51–75, 434th BS 76–99.

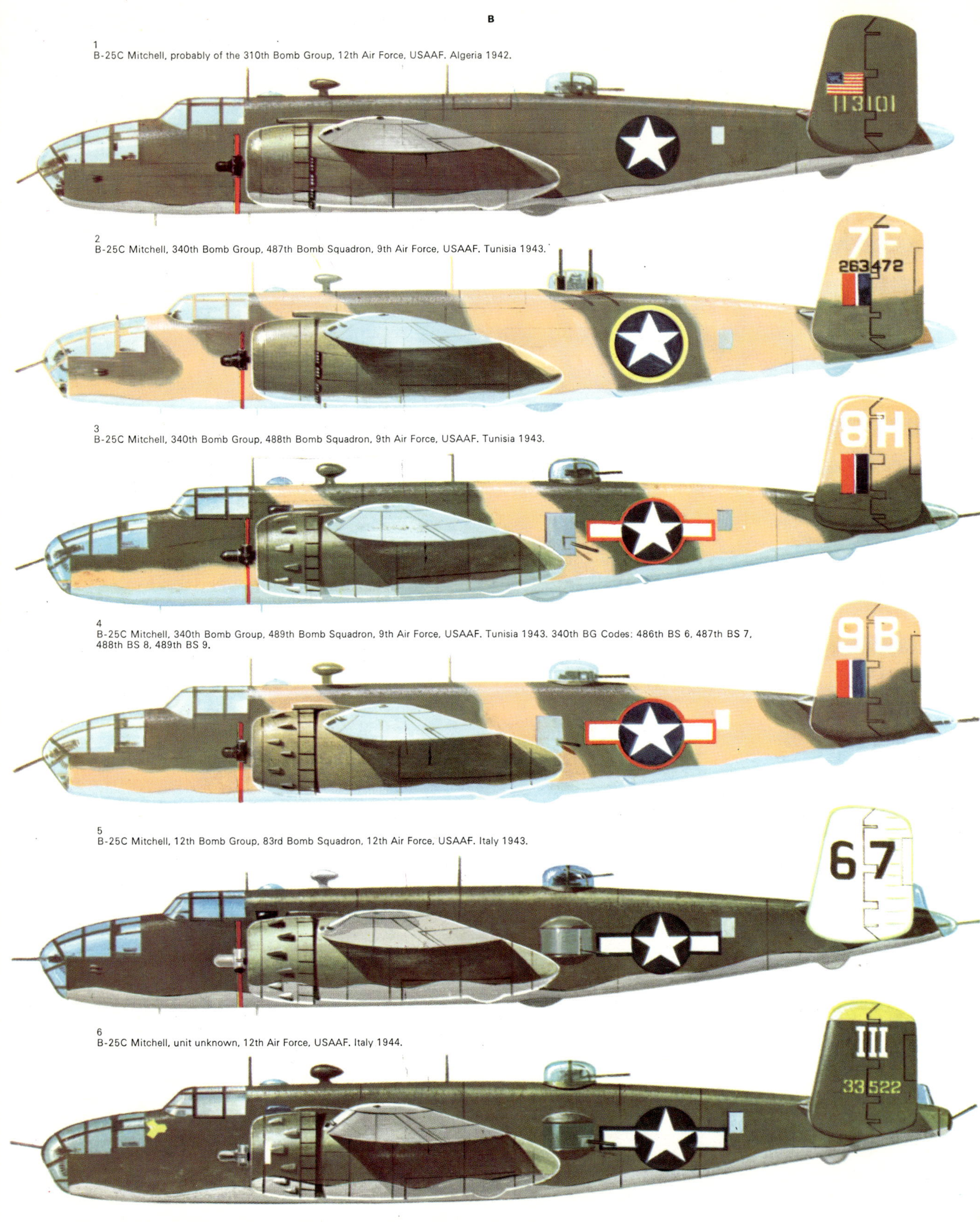

B

1
B-25C Mitchell, probably of the 310th Bomb Group, 12th Air Force, USAAF. Algeria 1942.

2
B-25C Mitchell, 340th Bomb Group, 487th Bomb Squadron, 9th Air Force, USAAF. Tunisia 1943.

3
B-25C Mitchell, 340th Bomb Group, 488th Bomb Squadron, 9th Air Force, USAAF. Tunisia 1943.

4
B-25C Mitchell, 340th Bomb Group, 489th Bomb Squadron, 9th Air Force, USAAF. Tunisia 1943. 340th BG Codes: 486th BS 6, 487th BS 7, 488th BS 8, 489th BS 9.

5
B-25C Mitchell, 12th Bomb Group, 83rd Bomb Squadron, 12th Air Force, USAAF. Italy 1943.

6
B-25C Mitchell, unit unknown, 12th Air Force, USAAF. Italy 1944.

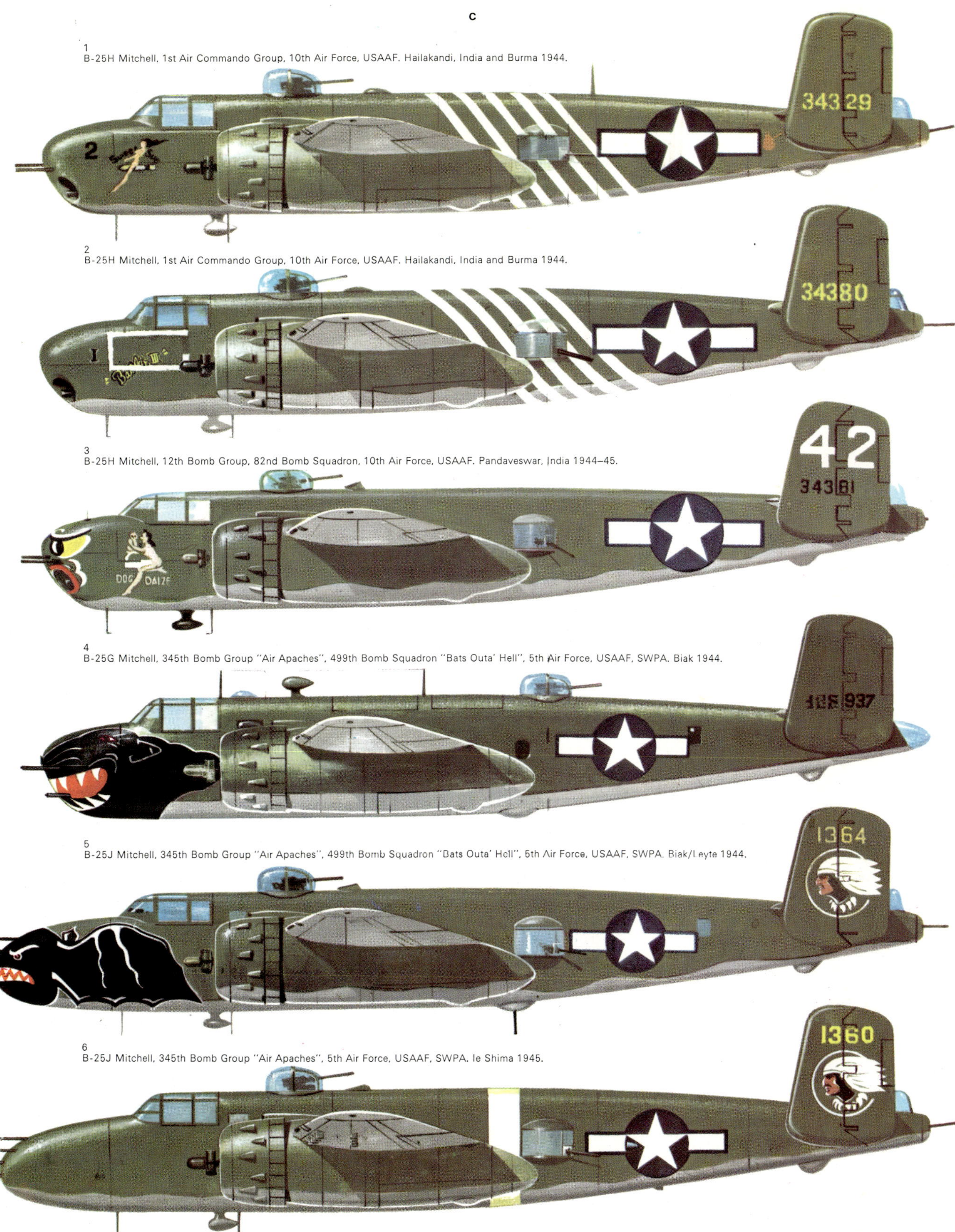

C

1
B-25H Mitchell, 1st Air Commando Group, 10th Air Force, USAAF. Hailakandi, India and Burma 1944.

2
B-25H Mitchell, 1st Air Commando Group, 10th Air Force, USAAF. Hailakandi, India and Burma 1944.

3
B-25H Mitchell, 12th Bomb Group, 82nd Bomb Squadron, 10th Air Force, USAAF. Pandaveswar, India 1944–45.

4
B-25G Mitchell, 345th Bomb Group "Air Apaches", 499th Bomb Squadron "Bats Outa' Hell", 5th Air Force, USAAF, SWPA. Biak 1944.

5
B-25J Mitchell, 345th Bomb Group "Air Apaches", 499th Bomb Squadron "Bats Outa' Hell", 5th Air Force, USAAF, SWPA. Biak/Leyte 1944.

6
B-25J Mitchell, 345th Bomb Group "Air Apaches", 5th Air Force, USAAF, SWPA. Ie Shima 1945.

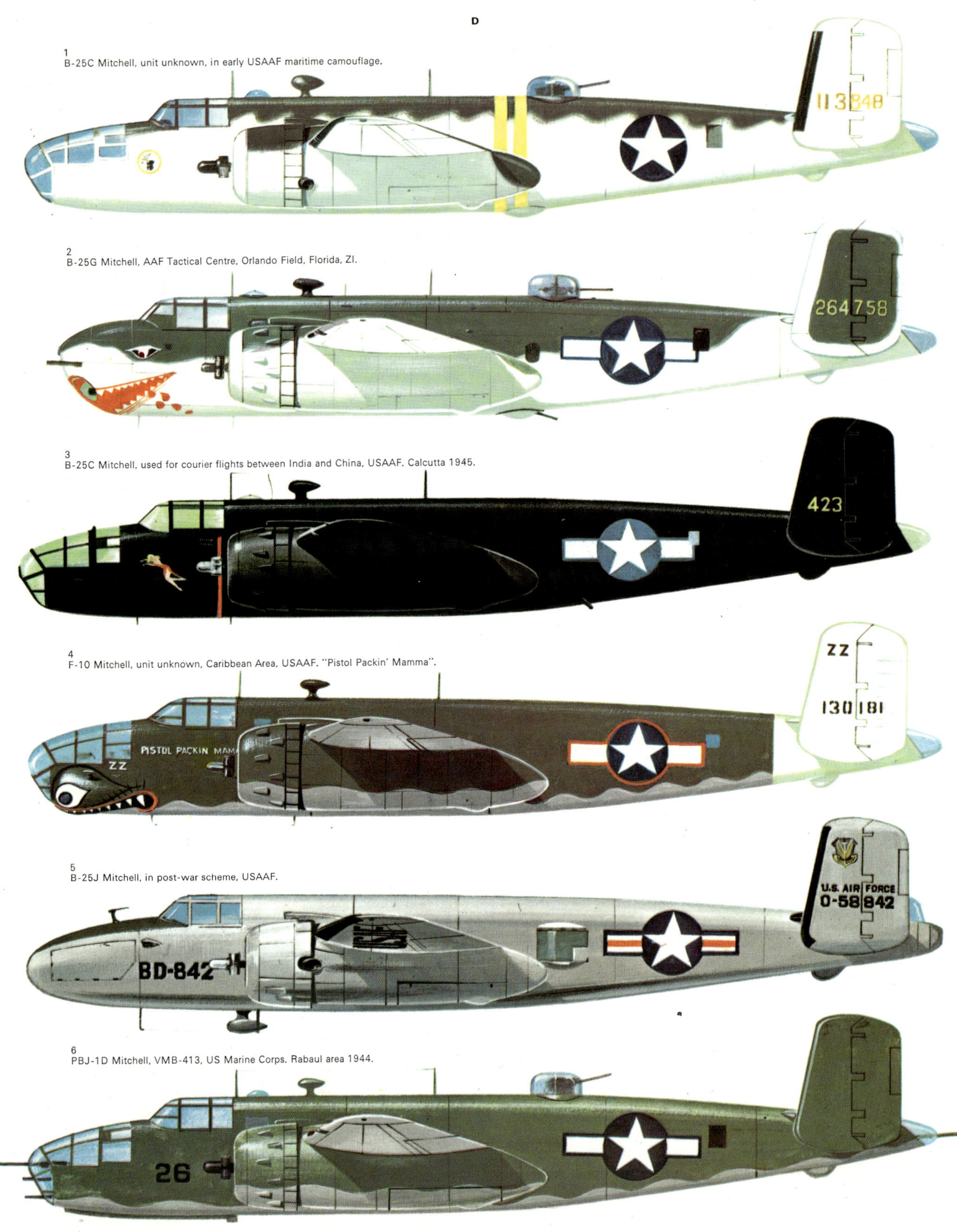

D

1
B-25C Mitchell, unit unknown, in early USAAF maritime camouflage.

2
B-25G Mitchell, AAF Tactical Centre, Orlando Field, Florida, ZI.

3
B-25C Mitchell, used for courier flights between India and China, USAAF. Calcutta 1945.

4
F-10 Mitchell, unit unknown, Caribbean Area, USAAF. "Pistol Packin' Mamma".

5
B-25J Mitchell, in post-war scheme, USAAF.

6
PBJ-1D Mitchell, VMB-413, US Marine Corps. Rabaul area 1944.

E

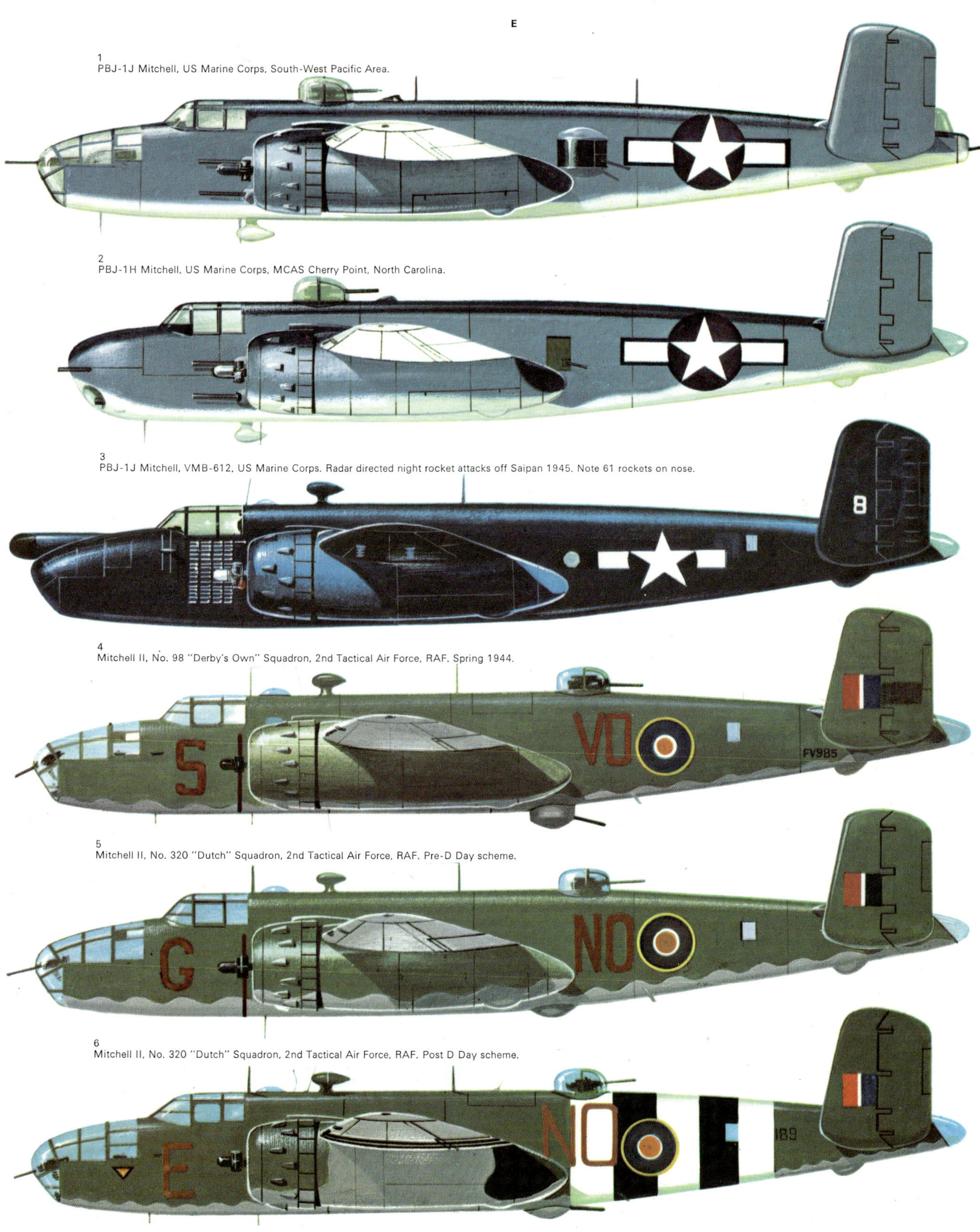

1
PBJ-1J Mitchell, US Marine Corps, South-West Pacific Area.

2
PBJ-1H Mitchell, US Marine Corps, MCAS Cherry Point, North Carolina.

3
PBJ-1J Mitchell, VMB-612, US Marine Corps. Radar directed night rocket attacks off Saipan 1945. Note 61 rockets on nose.

4
Mitchell II, No. 98 "Derby's Own" Squadron, 2nd Tactical Air Force, RAF. Spring 1944.

5
Mitchell II, No. 320 "Dutch" Squadron, 2nd Tactical Air Force, RAF. Pre-D Day scheme.

6
Mitchell II, No. 320 "Dutch" Squadron, 2nd Tactical Air Force, RAF. Post D Day scheme.

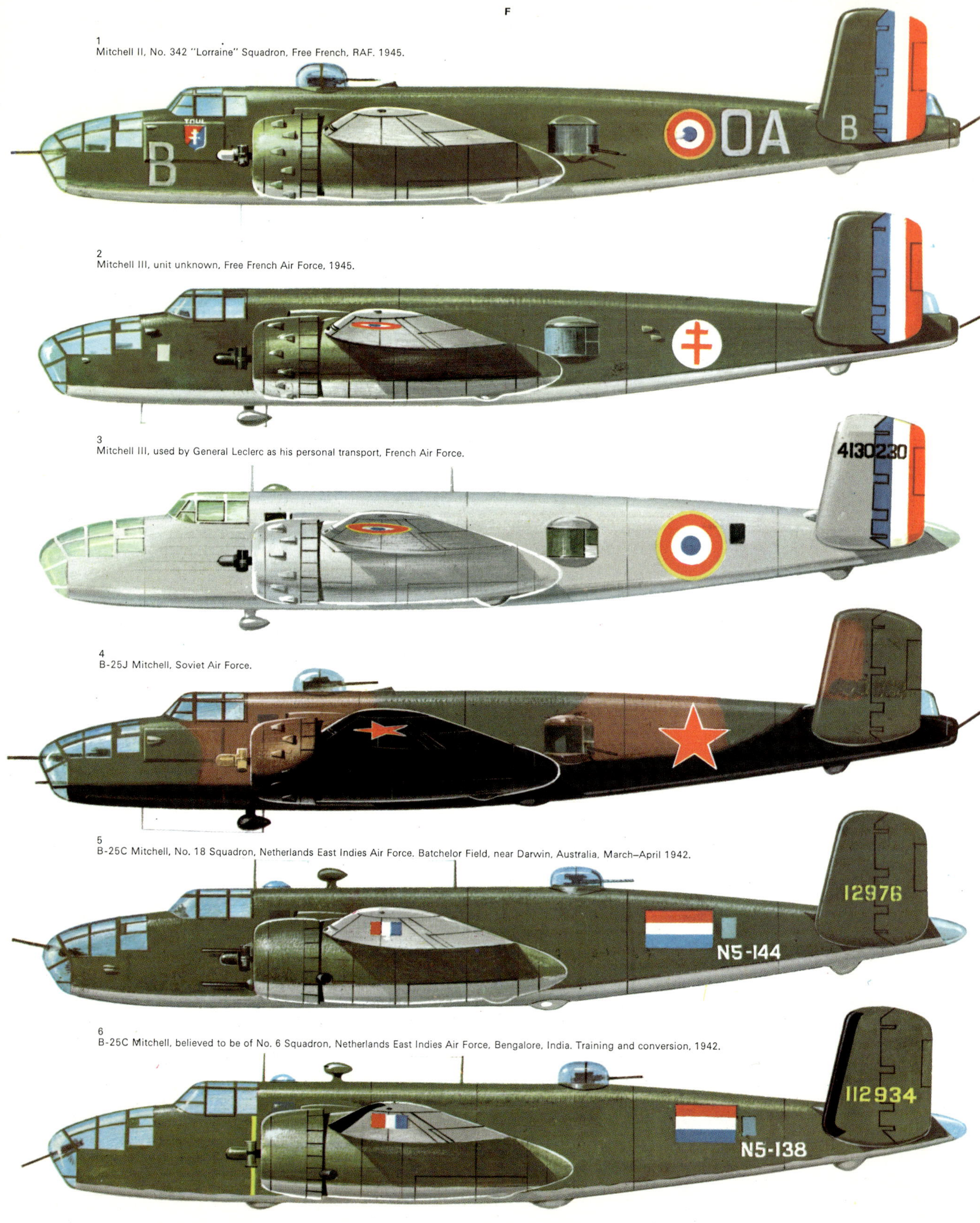

F

1
Mitchell II, No. 342 "Lorraine" Squadron, Free French, RAF. 1945.

2
Mitchell III, unit unknown, Free French Air Force, 1945.

3
Mitchell III, used by General Leclerc as his personal transport, French Air Force.

4
B-25J Mitchell, Soviet Air Force.

5
B-25C Mitchell, No. 18 Squadron, Netherlands East Indies Air Force. Batchelor Field, near Darwin, Australia, March–April 1942.

6
B-25C Mitchell, believed to be of No. 6 Squadron, Netherlands East Indies Air Force, Bengalore, India. Training and conversion, 1942.

1
B-25J Mitchell, No. 18 Squadron, Netherlands East Indies Air Force. Tjilitan, Bandoeng, Java 1947.

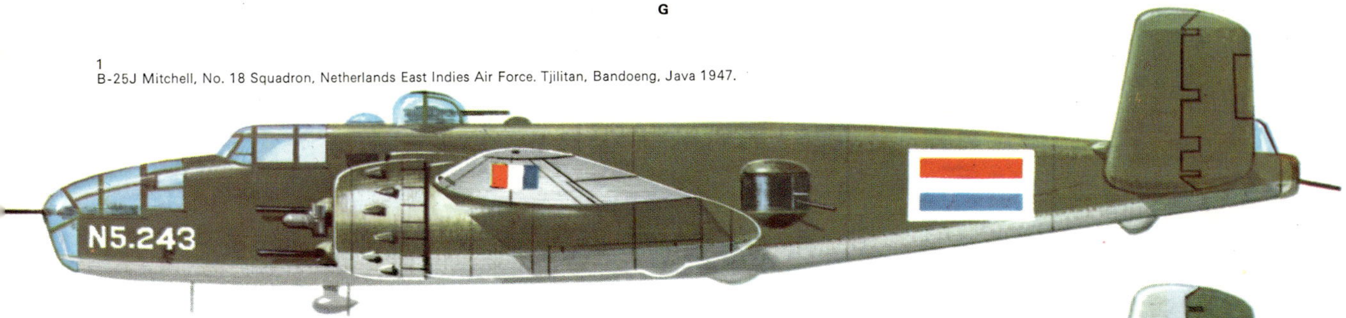

2
B-25J Mitchell, No. 18 Squadron, Netherlands East Indies Air Force, Tjilitan, Bandoeng, Java 1947.

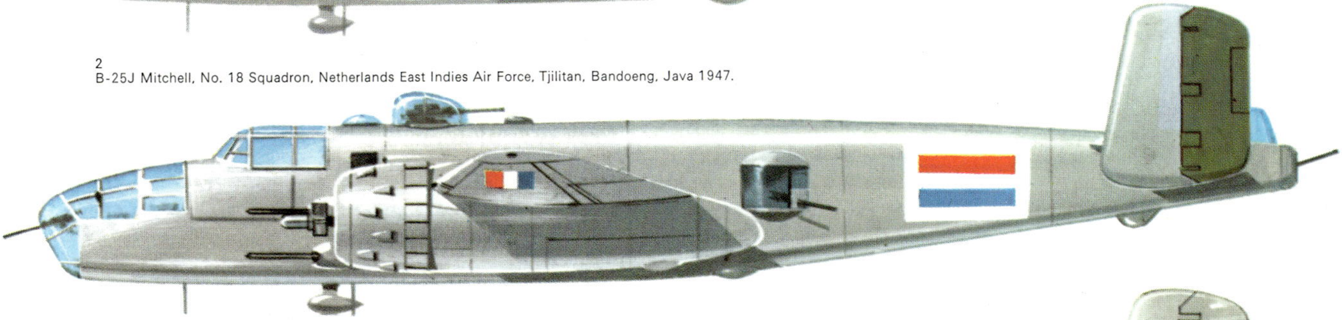

3
B-25J Mitchell, No. 18 Squadron, Netherlands East Indies Air Force, Tjilitan, Bandoeng, Java 1948.

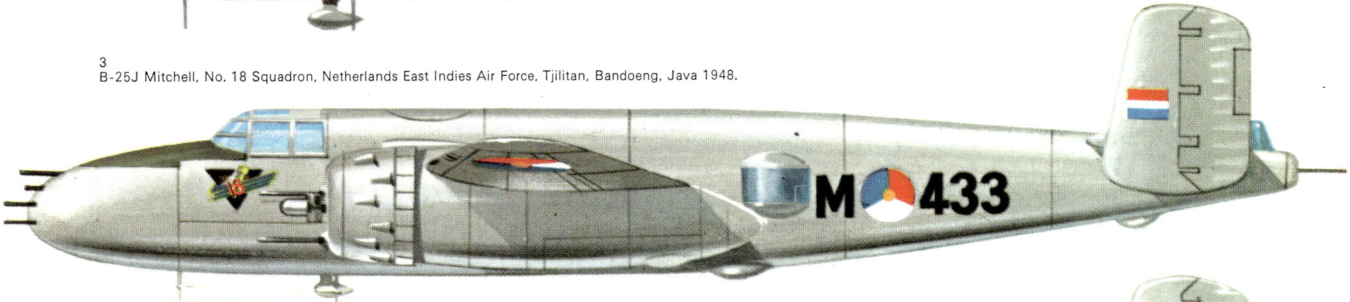

4
B-25J Mitchell, No. 18 Squadron, Netherlands East Indies Air Force, Tjilitan, Bandoeng, Java 1948.

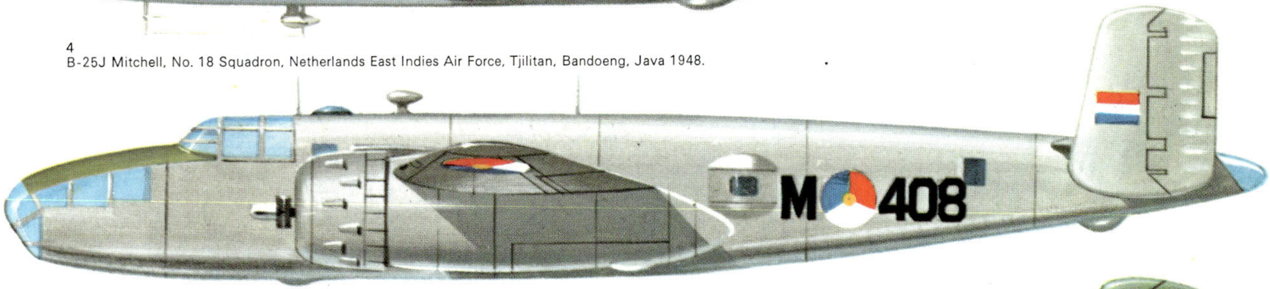

5
B-25C Mitchell, No. 320 Squadron, Kon. Marine. Valkenburg. In temporary scheme.

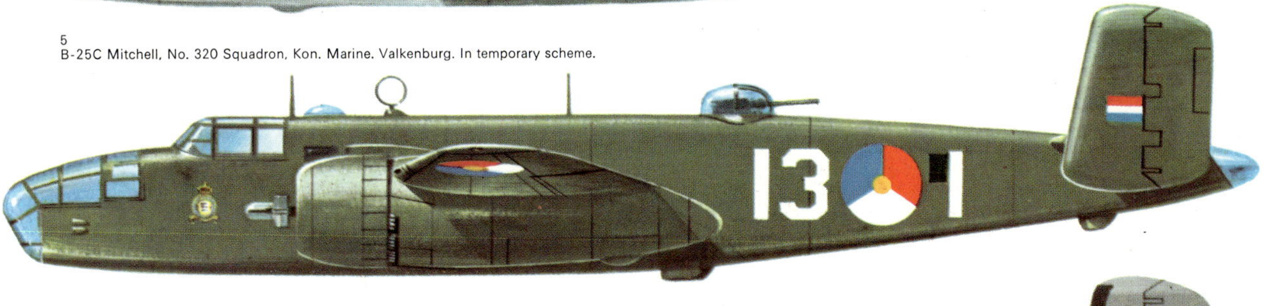

6
B-25C Mitchell, No. 320 Squadron, Kon. Marine. Valkenburg 1949.

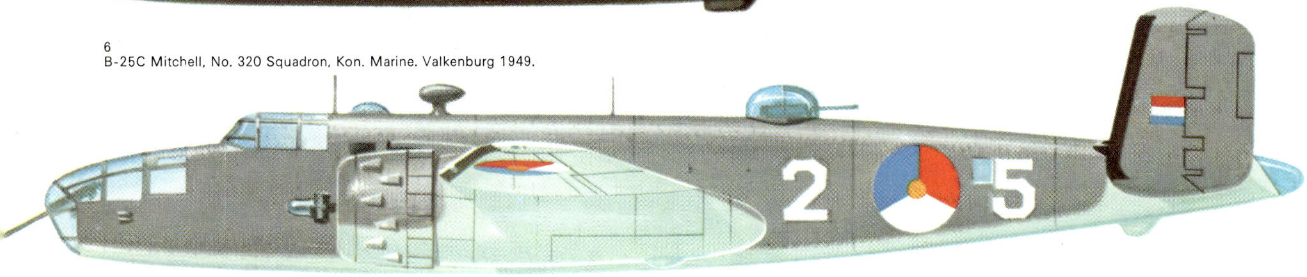

H

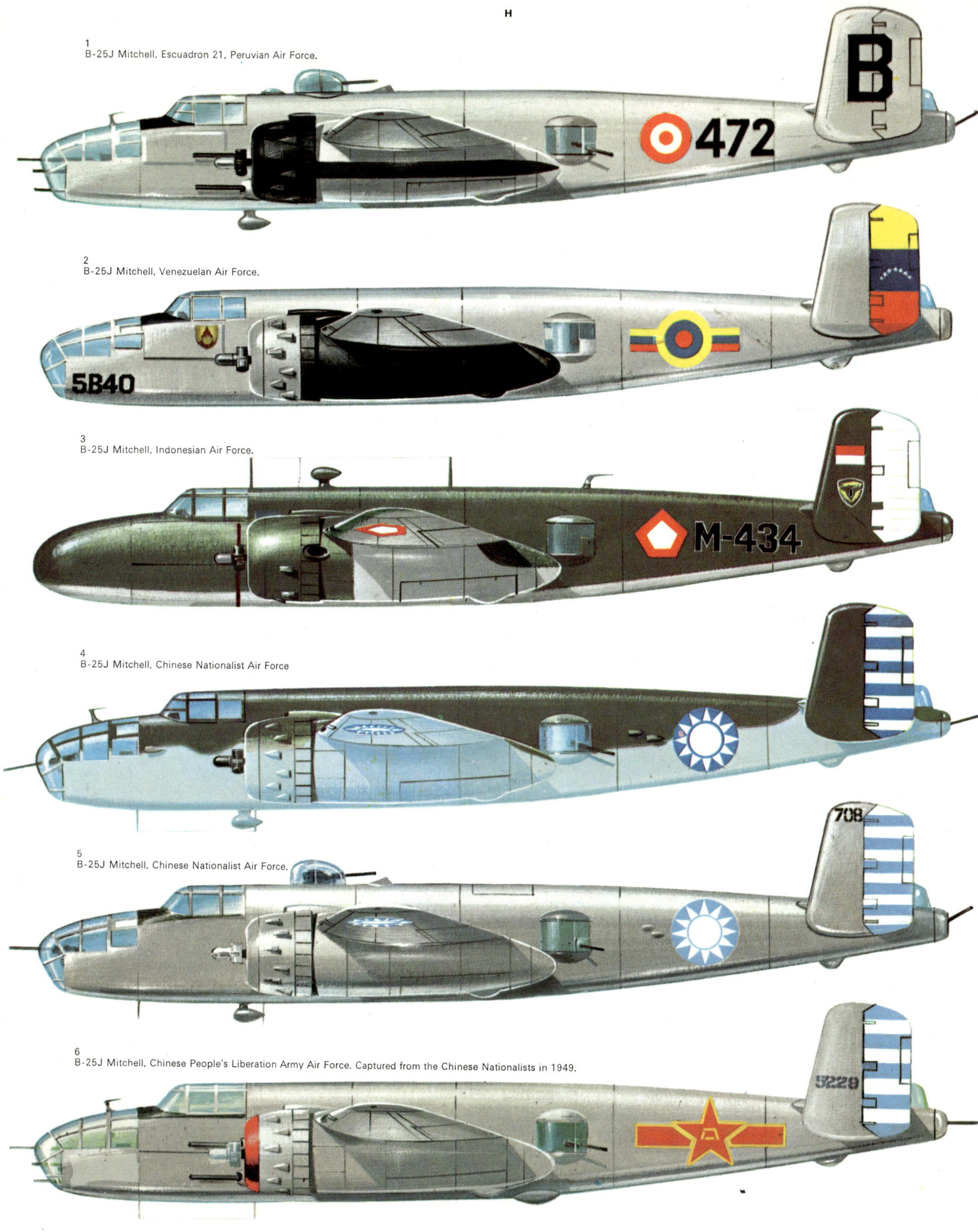

1
B-25J Mitchell, Escuadron 21, Peruvian Air Force.

2
B-25J Mitchell, Venezuelan Air Force.

3
B-25J Mitchell, Indonesian Air Force.

4
B-25J Mitchell, Chinese Nationalist Air Force

5
B-25J Mitchell, Chinese Nationalist Air Force.

6
B-25J Mitchell, Chinese People's Liberation Army Air Force. Captured from the Chinese Nationalists in 1949.

Above: B-25C's of the 345th Bomb Group, 499th Bomb Squadron, 5th Air Force, SWPA, supporting the Marine attack on Cape Gloucester, New Britain, December 1943.

Above: B-25J stripped of all armament on an Indian airfield in 1945. 345th Bomb Group. (Peter M. Bowers)

B-25H's with top armament removed of the 38th Bomb Group, 5th Air Force, SWPA, probably on Biak airfield during late 1944. (USAF)

Above: B-25H Mitchells of the 38th Bomb Group, 5th AF, SWPA, giving Jap installations on Dobo, Dutch New Guinea, a pounding on the 26 May 1944. (USAF)

Above: A couple of Mitchells, part of the Allied force which destroyed a 22 ship Japanese convoy during the Battle of the Bismark Sea, coming in on their bomb run at mast height. The Japs lost 12 troop transports (15,000 soldiers) and 10 cruisers and destroyers. 5th Air Force Mitchells, unit unknown; photo taken from a RAAF aircraft. (USAF)

Below: Mitchells of an unknown unit bombing Jap shipping in Hong Kong harbour. (USAF)

Above: Overall matt black courier B-25C used on the India-China run photographed at Calcutta, September 1945. (Peter M. Bowers)

Above: B-25J modified in post-war markings. (Peter M. Bowers)

Right: A Mitchell in rather unusual markings, a TB-25N of the Minnesota Air National Guard.

Below: A very colourful post-war Mitchell, colours are reputed to have been red fuselage stripes, engine nacelles and tail fins. (Peter M. Bowers)

Above: A pair of Corsairs formating with a Marine PBJ-1D Mitchell from MCAS El Centro, California. (US Marines)

Below: PBJ-1D Mitchell of VMB-413, the first USMC squadron in combat in the Rabaul-Keviang area on 15th March 1944. Standard OD and grey scheme. (US Marines)

Below: A formation of PBJ-1J Mitchells of VMB-443 on a training flight from Emirau MCAS, Emirau Island. Scheme appears to be overall pale grey. Note four fixed ·5's in nose. (US Marines)

Above: PBJ-1D Mitchell of VMB-413 "The Flying Nightmares" on one of the first raids of the type in the Rabaul area, March 1944. (US Marines)

Below: PBJ-1H Mitchell, US Marines, in Navy three-tone camouflage, MCAS Cherry Point, North Carolina. (US Marines)

Below: Line-up of Marine PBJ-1J bombers awaiting the take-off signal on a Pacific airstrip, aircraft are in the three-tone Navy scheme. (US Marines)

Above: Formation of RAF Mitchells bombing the marshalling yards at Dorsten. (IWM)

Below: Mitchell II's of No. 320 (Dutch) Squadron, No. 139 Wing, RAF, having the snow scrubbed off them at Melsbroek during the winter of 1944-45. (IWM)

Above: A pair of Mitchell II's of No. 98 Squadron, RAF, bombing a strong-point at Haveadorp, near Arnhem on 10 April 1945. (IWM)

Above: A No. 320 (Dutch) Squadron Mitchell II in full D-Day markings bombing a target in France shortly after D-Day. (IWM)

Below: Mitchell II of No. 320 (Dutch) Squadron, No. 139 Wing, 2nd Tactical Air Force, RAF.

Above: A Mitchell II of No. 226 Squadron, RAF, shortly after D-Day, heading out over a Channel convoy for targets in France. (IWM)

Above & below: Mitchell II's of No. 98 Squadron on bombing raids over France during 1944. (R. A. Brown)

Above & below: Mitchell II's of No. 320 (Dutch) Squadron being bombed-up, note the orange triangle under the front cockpit of S and single fixed ·5 in the nose. (IWM)

Below, left: A Mitchell III of No. 2 Squadron, RAAF, taking off from Livingstone bound for Morotai as the navigating aircraft for No. 457 Squadron's Spitfire Mk. VIII's upon their departure from the mainland for the Islands.

Below, right: A Mitchell III of No. 2 Squadron, Royal Australian Air Force, on Hughes Field, Northern Territory, June 1944. No. 2 Squadron code was KO but neither a/c letter or serial are known. (F. F. Smith)

Above & below: Mitchell II's of No. 342 "Lorraine" (Free French) Squadron, standard OD and grey scheme. (ECA via J. Cuny)

Below: Close-up of the nose of X KJ687. (Groupe Lorraine via J. Cuny)

Above: Mitchell II, Free French Air Force, unit unknown, on a North African airfield. (J. Cuny)

Above: Mitchell III in natural metal finish, French Air Force. (ECA via J. Cuny)

Below: The Mitchell III used by General Leclerc as his personal transport. (J. Cuny)

Above: B-25C Mitchell, No. 18 Squadron, Netherlands East Indies Air Force, Batchelor Field, Darwin, Australia during 1942.

Left: Line-up of B-25C's of No. 18 Squadron, Batchelor Field. No. 18 Squadron trained at Batchelor Field near Darwin and No. 6 Squadron at Bengalore, India.
(via F. F. Smith)

Below: B-25J Mitchells of No. 18 Squadron, NEIAF on Tjilitan airfield, Java. All aircraft with top turrets removed. (Hugo Hooftman)

Below: Nose detail of a B-25J of No. 18 Squadron, note the transparent panels have all been overpainted in silver or black with the exception of the small one in the nose. (Hugo Hooftman)

Above: Formation of B-25J's of No. 18 Squadron, note black and white codes and return to the pre-war national insignia. (R.Neth.AF)

Above: B-25C in post-war markings, NEIAF.

Below: Good flying shot of M408, probably taken in 1947, note overpainting of top of nose glass-house. (R.Neth.AF)

Above: B-25C of No. 320 Squadron, Royal Netherlands Navy. These aircraft were originally on the strength of No. 320 (Dutch) Squadron, RAF during the war. About ten B-25C's were operated by No. 320 Squadron Kon. Marine, originally numbered from 13-1 onwards but later changed to 2-1 onwards. This photo shows engine nacelle and nose painting details very clearly. Grey and sky scheme. (R.Neth.AF)

Left: B-25C 2-2 in grey and sky scheme. (B. van der Klaauw)

Above: 13-1 in the short-lived overall olive green scheme. Note KON.MARINE in small white letters under tail-plane. (R.Neth.AF)

Below: 2-5 in grey and sky scheme with 2-5 apparently in overall OD scheme in background. Note KON.MARINE in black under tail-plane. (R.Neth.AF)

Above: An ex-NEIAF B-25J in the colours and markings of the Indonesian Air Force. (S. P. Peltz)

Right: An unarmed B–25C of the Chinese Nationalist Air Force, probably used as a photo-recce aircraft.

Below: Natural metal B-25J of the Chinese Nationalist Air Force. (Peter M. Bowers)

Below: B-25J's and C-46's of the Chinese People's Liberation Army Air Force captured from the Chinese Nationalists in 1949.

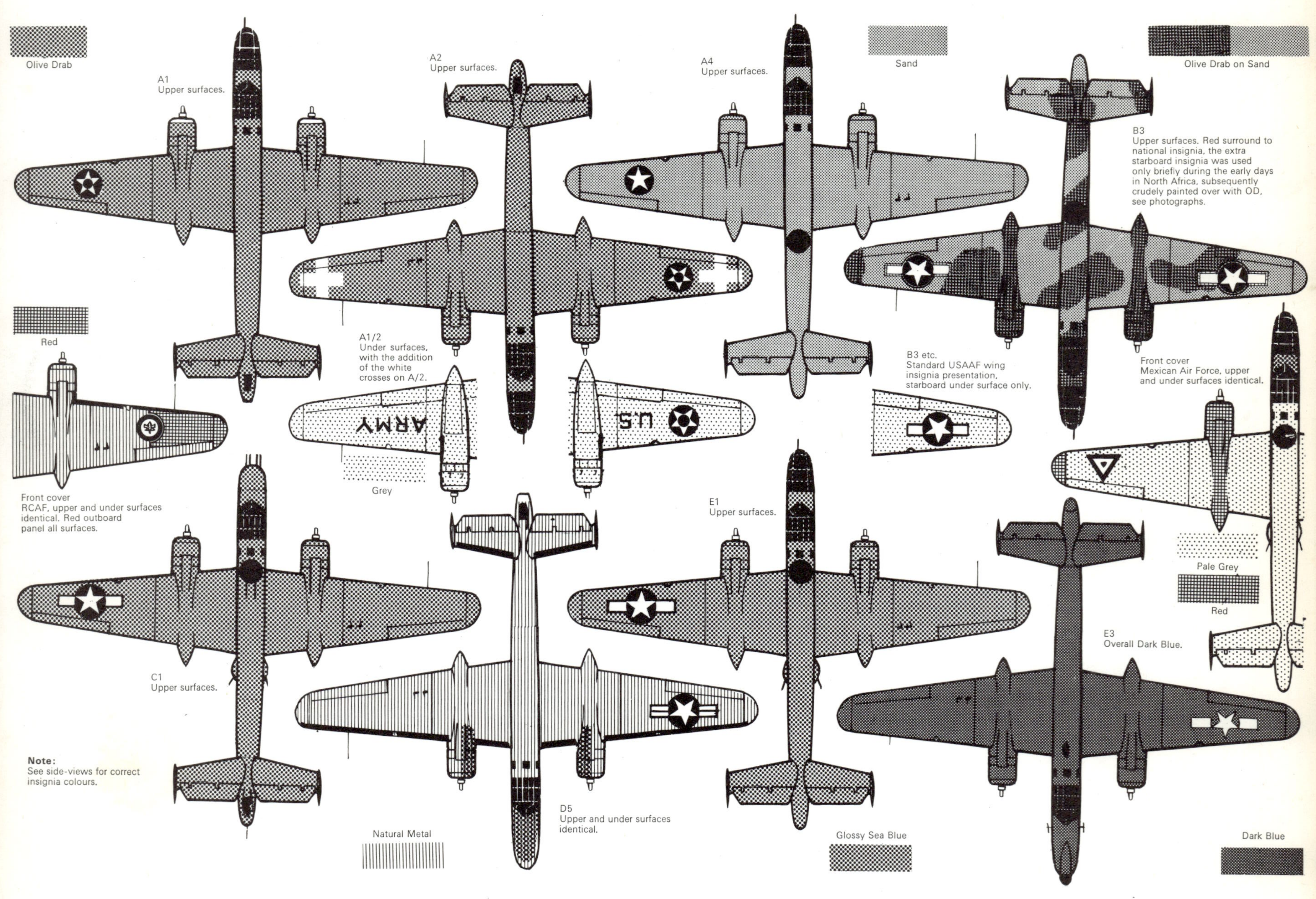
Olive Drab
A1
Upper surfaces.
A2
Upper surfaces.
A4
Upper surfaces.
Sand
Olive Drab on Sand
B3
Upper surfaces. Red surround to national insignia, the extra starboard insignia was used only briefly during the early days in North Africa, subsequently crudely painted over with OD, see photographs.
Red
A1/2
Under surfaces, with the addition of the white crosses on A/2.
ARMY
U.S
Grey
B3 etc.
Standard USAAF wing insignia presentation, starboard under surface only.
Front cover
Mexican Air Force, upper and under surfaces identical.
Front cover
RCAF, upper and under surfaces identical. Red outboard panel all surfaces.
E1
Upper surfaces.
Pale Grey
Red
E3
Overall Dark Blue.
C1
Upper surfaces.
Note:
See side-views for correct insignia colours.
D5
Upper and under surfaces identical.
Natural Metal
Glossy Sea Blue
Dark Blue